BBC
RADIO
4

Prayers
To See You
Through
Each Day

WATKINS
Sharing Wisdom Since
1893

This edition published in the UK and USA in 2017 by
Watkins, an imprint of Watkins Media Limited
19 Cecil Court
London WC2N 4EZ

enquiries@watkinspublishing.co.uk

By arrangement with the BBC
The BBC logo is a trade mark of the British Broadcasting Corporation and
is used under licence.
BBC logo copyright © BBC 2005
Radio 4 logo copyright © Radio 4 2011

Design and typography copyright © Watkins Media Limited 2017
Foreword copyright © Catherine Wybourne 2017
Text from the BBC Radio 4 series *Prayer for the Day* copyright © BBC
2007–2016

The prayers in this book were first published by Watkins in *Prayer for the
Day Volume I* in 2014 and in *Prayer for the Day Volume II* in 2016.

9 8 7 6 5 4 3 2 1

Designed and typeset by Glen Wilkins

Printed and bound in Europe

A CIP record for this book is available from the British Library

ISBN: 978-1-78678-076-8

www.watkinspublishing.com

CONTENTS

FOREWORD

by *Sister Catherine Wybourne*

What is prayer? The old Catholic catechism definition, a raising up of the heart and mind to God, captures prayer's matter-of-factness, its ordinariness and its extraordinary scope, for it takes us into the hidden places of God. I like, too, the poet George Herbert's phrase 'the heart in pilgrimage', because prayer is about seeking God, which can never be a casual quest nor one in which the mind alone takes part.

To pray we sometimes need words, above all the words of scripture or the liturgy, or the inspiring words of men and women like those in this book, who enable us to see with fresh eyes. More often we need silence: the profound, attentive silence St Benedict writes about in his Rule – which, paradoxically, can co-exist with less than perfect physical silence. Indeed, a little noise, a 'distraction' or two, can be helpful. They remind us that prayer is not all about us. It is not a retreat from the 'real' world, where the two superpowers – God and us – meet. It is, in fact, a deeper engagement with reality, where faith alone can sustain us.

Prayer is not always consoling, any more than life itself is. It can be bleak; it can be challenging. And if we are truly open to God, we can also be open to everything that is opposed to God. There is thus a risk inherent in prayer. The biggest risk probably comes from our wanting to do all the talking, which can lead us away from God into a hell of our own making, although we may not recognize it as such. Not every seemingly good idea comes from God, nor do any which are destructive of ourselves or others.

What is the best way to pray? The simple answer is as we can, not as we can't. But experience suggests there are ways of making prayer as natural to us as breathing. Regularity is important: better to pray for a few minutes each day than struggle to pray for an hour or more every now and then. Finding somewhere uncluttered is also a help, as is prayer in the early morning before the day's business fills our thoughts. God wants us to pray, to spend time with Him. However hard prayer may seem at times, however reluctant we may be to pray, we must remember that God has already poured the gift of prayer into our hearts. He loves us and asks nothing in return but our love.

We should never be afraid of honesty in prayer or think we have to be 'good' for our prayer to be acceptable. The psalms are full of curses, doubt, pain and hopelessness as well as thanksgiving and praise. They mirror our own condition exactly. I hope it is not too fanciful to see *Prayers To See You Through Each Day* as a kind of psalter for our times. It encourages me, as I hope it will encourage you, to cultivate that 'simple, naked intent unto God' which is prayer.

Sister Catherine Wybourne is Prioress of the Benedictine monastery Holy Trinity at Howton Grove, Hereford. She is known to her thousands of social media followers as 'Digitalnun'.

The Day's Adventure

From the moment our eyes open on a new dawn to the time our heads hit the pillow, each day provides many opportunities for deepening our relationship with God. This chapter begins with a prayer for the early morning and concludes with one for sleep, offering in between reflections for an array of human situations, such as a prayer for living mindfully in the present, another on the need to wait patiently, and a meditation on using our speech to heal rather than hurt. These prayers show how, with God's help, our days can be times of healing, belonging, laughter and love, through the ordinary circumstances of our lives.

On Beginning Again

Michael Ford

The Reverend Dr Michael Ford, a former BBC journalist, is an author of books on contemporary Christian spirituality. He is a specialist in the work of the Dutch pastoral theologian Henri JM Nouwen.

The Spanish mystic St John of the Cross says the soul at dawn is like a sparrow on a rooftop, turning itself toward the Spirit of Love.

It's a poetic image. Each day is an opportunity to renew our lives before God: to put the past behind us and reorient ourselves using the divine compass.

I like the description of a Christian as someone who says, 'Today I am beginning again', a statement that finds its source in the Resurrection of Christ. No sin, no mistake, no regret has the last word as we focus on the mercy of God rather than those things that plague us with feelings of guilt or shame. God is no tormentor of the human conscience.

Each day we're encouraged to set off again along a spiritual path which will never be devoid of trial or temptation. This is what conversion is all about: to begin again without fear. The Christian life can only be understood in terms of continually renewed conversion. And in this respect our lives become literally revolutionized.

Revolution comes from the Latin, *revolutus*, to turn around. Christianity is about turning around again and again. In the words of Gregory of Nyssa, in the Christian life we go forward 'from beginning to beginning, across beginnings that never end'.

Creator God,

as this new day dawns,

may the morning star rise in our hearts

to bring us the light of life

and lead us toward the everlasting day.

Amen.

On Finding Ways of
Praising Others

Krish Kandiah

Dr Krish Kandiah is the founder and director of 'Home for Good', a charity helping vulnerable children. A vice-president of Tear Fund, he is the author of ten books, including the award-winning Paradoxology.

Right now, parents and carers around the country are trying to grab a few more precious moments of sleep before they're dragged kicking and screaming into consciousness by a child desperate to go out into the cold and do some kicking and screaming of their own. While most of us are still in our pyjamas, there is a dedicated minority who have an icy start to the day, struggling to keep warm on a touchline.

I've seen some of the benefits of early-morning football training with my birth children, but it was with one particular foster son that I really witnessed the transforming power of sport. He'd had a difficult start to life and struggled with almost everything – concentrating, coordinating, anxiety attacks, poor eyesight, socializing and behaviour. I took him to burn off some energy, and as the coaches invested time and attention in him, he grew in confidence and self-esteem – precious things for a young footballer likely to spend his entire childhood in the care system.

Unlike Bill Shankly, I'm not convinced that football is more serious than life or death, but I do believe sport can be a force for good in the world. For my foster son, sport was the stage for kind words to be spoken. Sport was the social context to receive a rare pat of affirmation, a cheer of celebration or an embrace of commiseration.

But praise needn't be confined to a cold field on a Saturday morning. Let's kickstart a new habit in life-building affirmation and practice today, commending those we rub shoulders with.

Lord God,

father to the fatherless,

protector of widows and orphans,

awaken us today to the opportunities

to offer kindness and hope

in the lives of those around us.

Amen.

On Finding Ways of Praising Others

On Using Our Speech for Good

Alison Murdoch

Alison Murdoch is the former Director of Jamyang Buddhist Centre, London, and of The Foundation for Developing Compassion and Wisdom. She is co-author of 16 Guidelines for a Happy Life.

I've always been drawn to the saying of King Solomon: 'death and life are in the power of the tongue.' Or as the comedian Eric Idle said more recently: 'sticks and stones may break my bones, but words will make me go in a corner and cry by myself for hours.'

This emphasis on the power of words is reflected in the Tibetan Buddhist equivalent of the Ten Commandments. Out of ten 'non-virtuous actions', four of them relate to the way we choose to speak: lying, gossip, harsh words and divisive speech.

The first time I heard this, it came as a wake-up call. Few of us would argue that lying is almost always wrong, but the other three are part of daily life. Gossip, harsh words and divisive speech are the bread and butter of the media, and programmes such as *The Apprentice* have turned them into mass entertainment.

This seems particularly sad when the capacity to master language is one of the special qualities that make us human. Every morning we wake up with a fresh choice: either to share the grumpy mood or hurtful remark that can spoil someone else's day; or else to consciously use our speech as a force for good – to show kindness and concern, to encourage and inspire. If we genuinely want to make the world a better place, paying attention to our use of words is a failsafe way to go about it.

Let us pray

that all of us can find a way to speak today

that will heal rather than hurt.

May we use the power of the tongue

with kindness and care.

May we find the strength to make this a habit,

day after day.

On Opening Our Minds

Leslie Griffiths

The Reverend Dr Leslie Griffiths, Lord Griffiths of Burry Port, is Superintendent of Wesley's Chapel and a Labour Life Peer. He served as President of the Methodist Conference from 1994 to 1995.

Memory's a strange and wonderful thing. Just consider this. A letter arrives in the post. I don't have to open it to know who it's from – the handwriting gives the game away. As soon as I see the envelope, I can picture the person who wrote it, someone who's known me since I was a child. At the very sight of it, warm and vivid memories flood into my mind. Before I start to read, I've been transported back in time. See what I mean?

And I could add so many examples to show the way apparently innocuous events are charged with the possibility of opening our minds, awakening us to old pleasures (or fears, of course) and reminding us that the past hasn't gone forever. It lurks barely below the rim of our consciousness, just waiting for its moment to greet us. It could be a place we pass through, a snatch of music we hear, someone's face, the bite of an apple – any one of so many things that releases an energy we didn't know existed.

ON OPENING OUR MINDS

It isn't that our minds stretch back to a disappearing past; it's more the past rising up to claim the present. I get this feeling every time I take bread and wine in a service of Holy Communion. 'This do in remembrance of me,' Jesus said, and those words do the trick every time. Time isn't just an ever-rolling stream that bears us all away. It's with us, in us, around us, bubbling away beneath the surface and always waiting to surprise us.

Dear Lord,

live with us today,

go with us into the day's work.

Give us a sense of Your abiding presence

with us in all we do.

We thank You for all that is past

and trust You for all that is to come.

Amen.

On Patient Waiting

Derek Boden

The Reverend Derek Boden was Presbyterian Chaplain to the University of Ulster in Coleraine, as well as Minister of Malone Presbyterian Church in Belfast.

This spring, in my part of Ireland, the whitethorn blossom came late. When the bloom did come, it came suddenly, and in what seemed like an instant a profusion of white-blossomed borders graced the roads and the fields. And those of us fortunate enough to have a thorn hedge in our gardens were garlanded with a wealth of creamy blossom. With that profusion of white bloom and with the beauty of the fresh green everywhere, our hard, long winter was forgotten.

If every waiting time brought such compensation, our waiting would be the more bearable. As it is, the waiting is hard to endure. Those test results, whether medical or academic, bring their own anxieties. Most of us don't deal well with the 'time between'. Between the planting and the blossom, between the sowing and the reaping, between the asking and the hearing, how interminable it all seems. How long, O Lord, how long!

On Patient Waiting

It was a line from TS Eliot that gave me pause for thought, as with so many other lines of his. In 'Choruses from The Rock', Eliot wrote of taking no thought of the harvest, but only of proper sowing. Good advice, but I'm afraid I'm a 'harvest' person, though as I get older the wisdom of Eliot and others makes me think.

So grant us, O Lord,

the patience to do just what lies to hand

and to trust that You in Your wisdom

will bring to fruition that which is already

of Your mind and Your heart.

Amen.

On Desire and Passion

Gemma Simmonds

Dr Gemma Simmonds CJ is a sister of the Congregation of Jesus.
She teaches theology at Heythrop College, London, and is a volunteer
Chaplain at Holloway Prison.

The poet Don Marquis had a character, Archy the cockroach, who is a natural philosopher. In the poem entitled 'The Moth', Archy reflects on the folly of a moth who is so attracted to light that he ends up burning himself in a light source. When Archy questions the sense of this suicidal attraction, the moth replies that he would rather live a short life of passionate beauty than a long one of boring sameness.

When the moth immolates himself on the bright blaze of a cigar lighter, Archy muses that he would rather settle for half the happiness and twice the longevity; but, he says, 'at the same time I wish / there was something I wanted / as badly as he wanted to fry himself.'

St Augustine of Hippo might be called the patron saint of desire. After all, he once wrote a prayer, 'Lord, give me chastity, but not yet.' He taught that being in touch with our deepest desires can lead us to the God who is the ultimate goal of all true desire. Archy the cockroach reflects that passionate desires can lead us into danger, but a life lived without passion is hardly worth living. It must be true passion, the longing for life's deepest potential, rather than pointless craving for trivialities. Perhaps the secret is to find deep joy and satisfaction in the quiet quality of living, as well as in the intense moments, embracing what one writer has called the 'Sacrament of the Present Moment'.

God of all moments,

both the quiet and the passionate,

teach us to seek and find You

at the heart of all our desires,

especially in each present moment,

since You are the end of all our longing.

Amen.

On Living Mindfully

Ian Bradley

The Very Reverend Dr Ian Bradley is Reader in Practical Theology and Church History at the University of St Andrews, where he is Principal of St Mary's College and a university Chaplain.

Mindfulness is one of the great mantras of our time. Bestselling books, CDs, apps and courses present it as a technique which will relieve anxiety, stress, irritation and tiredness.

At its heart is an emphasis on resting in clear awareness of the present moment and allowing yourself to be just as you are. Mindfulness meditation focuses on breathing and on recognizing when the mind has wandered. When this happens, there's no recrimination or rebuke but the mind is led gently back to the breath. Thoughts, especially those that dwell on regrets about the past or fears about the future, are treated as clouds passing across the sky.

Something close to mindfulness is at the heart of Christianity. In his Sermon on the Mount, Jesus told the crowds who'd gathered to hear him not to worry about their lives. He commended the birds of the air and the flowers of the fields for not fretting about what they are going to eat or wear. This isn't the only time that he urged his followers to live in the present and not dwell in the past or worry about the future. When one of his disciples asked to be allowed to go off and bury his father before following him, Jesus famously retorted, 'Follow me, and leave the dead to bury the dead.'

Many great Christian mystics over the ages have developed techniques of meditation similarly aimed at freeing their minds from distraction.

Merciful God,

You understand all, forgive all,

absorb and encompass all.

Teach us not to dwell on the past

or be filled with fear for the future

but rather to live fully in the present,

breathing in time with Your divine breath

and spirit.

Amen.

On Being Grateful

Edward Mason

The Reverend Prebendary Edward Mason was appointed Rector of Bath Abbey in 2004. In 2015 he was appointed Honorary Chaplain to the Queen.

I don't think I can recall another time in my life when money has been in the news so much. Throughout the day we're told about the FTSE and late at night I'm reassured – or worried – to hear how Wall Street closed. Now, I know these days following biting recession continue to be hard. Many will feel vulnerable to redundancy, homes are under threat and income from savings is perilously low. It's tough out there – especially for someone whose source of income has actually dried up.

But, if we're not careful, money can dominate every moment and make us lesser human beings.

I once knew someone who would say, 'It's only money.' This usually came up when something important and costly had to be bought or paid for. We all know it can be hard – even for those of us that have enough – to write the cheques for kids' university fees, pay for a holiday or buy that birthday present. We can become quite stingy and hand over the money grudgingly. So it's helpful to remind ourselves that 'it's only money' and that there are far more valuable things around.

In the Bible, there's a letter that St Paul wrote to people who were experiencing tough times. He says, 'Be joyful always, pray continually; give thanks in all circumstances.' He knew that being grateful – even in the testing times – puts us in touch with God and a better life.

So, Lord God,

I thank You for giving me life today.

Help me to foster good and loving

relationships in my community and,

if I start to let money become more important

than people, help me to remember,

'It's only money.'

Amen.

On Being Architects of Our Future

Dónal McKeown

The Most Reverend Dr Dónal McKeown was appointed Roman Catholic Bishop of Derry in 2014. For 23 years he was a teacher, including as Principal of St Malachy's College in Belfast.

I went to secondary school for the first time about three weeks after the Berlin Wall was erected. Mind you, that particular fact wasn't on my mind as I began my first lessons in German. However, during the course of many visits to that country over nearly 30 years, I worked on the common assumption that the so-called Iron Curtain – and its bizarre division of Berlin – were just part of the normal run of things. Immutable powers had divided Europe into camps and we had to accept that fact. The nightmare does not want us to dream.

But then, on 9 November 1989, brave, crazy dreamers marched and the walls came tumbling down. Within a decade of the fall of the Wall, we had tragedy in the former Yugoslavia – but also saw the end of apartheid in South Africa, and the Belfast Agreement.

We all have to live with the realities of life – but what we take to be normal can sometimes blind us to latent possibilities. It takes the vision of some to help others believe that change and growth are possible.

Many will rise this morning, worried about work and finances, burdens and bills. Some will have major decisions to make. We may be partially prisoners of our personal and communal past – but we are also capable of being audacious architects of our future. That future will belong to those who dare to dream of healing, community, laughter and love. To dream of anything less is to do an injustice to ourselves and our potential.

Lord,

Today is full of challenges and possibilities.

Help me to believe that we are all capable

of great little things.

And in that belief, help me to chip away

at the harsh cold walls

That disfigure the face of humankind which

was made in Your image and likeness.

Amen.

On the Renewal of Sleep

Mark Coffey

*Mark Coffey is a teacher of religion and philosophy at the Manchester
Grammar School, and a regular presenter of* The Daily Service *on
Radio 4.*

'Fatigue,' said Benjamin Franklin, 'is the best pillow.' Apparently rats sleep for up to 14 hours a day, while elephants and giraffes need only three to four hours a night – that's an hour's less kip than Winston Churchill's reported average, though he was an advocate of the afternoon nap.

Aware that, by definition, one cannot consciously enjoy the sensation of sleeping, the philosopher Montaigne had his servant wake him in his château so that he could have a good go at it as he fell asleep all over again. Marcel Proust had the first part of his classic work *In Search of Lost Time* rejected by publishers for taking 30 pages to describe the observations of an insomniac trying to get to sleep. And the Bible even records one Eutychus falling out of a window as he dozed off during a sermon of St Paul. Fortunately, the apostolic prayers were heard and he recovered.

Neurological studies have observed volunteer sleepers in brain scanners, and there is some evidence to suggest that as the mind relaxes, a process of clearing up the clutter of our emotions from the previous day goes on. So there's every reason to cut the caffeine intake, get right away from the PC and relax with a good read, or even Radio 4, before you hit the hay.

In our hectic world of apparently ever-increasing productivity, there's a wisdom in the words of Jesus who said, 'Do not worry about tomorrow, for tomorrow will worry about itself. Each day has enough trouble of its own.'

Eternally watchful God

who never sleeps or slumbers,

we thank You for the gift of sleep;

for its renewal and the reminder that,

mercifully, there are limitations on the

demands of each day.

Amen.

LET NOTHING DISTURB YOU

We all have tough experiences at times and need to
draw upon our spiritual reserves to get through them.
This chapter is a collection of prayers for moments
when we ask for God's love, strength and wisdom to
see our way more clearly and hopefully. The situations
range from truly dark experiences of loss and despair
to simple mistakes from which we can learn and grow.
There are prayers here to help us confront our own
anger and convert it to energy for righting wrongs; to
remind us, when we feel empty, of life's meaning and
purpose; and to offer us, when daunted or defeated,
an energizing jolt of courage or resolve.

On Owning Our Problems

Alison Murdoch

Alison Murdoch is the former Director of Jamyang Buddhist Centre, London, and of The Foundation for Developing Compassion and Wisdom. She is co-author of 16 Guidelines for a Happy Life.

In my Christmas stocking last year I found a fridge magnet. It's headed 'Libra' – which is my star sign – with the comments: 'manipulative, flighty, indecisive, impatient, gullible and sulky. Escapist, extravagant, flirtatious ...', and so on. Instead of a set of scales, there's a woman trying to juggle shopping bags and cupcakes. It brings a smile, and hits the mark much more effectively than the usual astrological flattery.

Santa Claus – or rather, my husband – has clearly mastered the art of indirect communication. It wouldn't have been so easy to say this to my face. On the other hand, I can see that the things that rub us up the wrong way are also the things that polish us. Before I got married, for example, I considered myself a model of patience and reason. Now, every morning, there's an upturned loo seat to remind me that I'm not. I can either lose my cool, or else use the loo seat as a gentle reminder that I've still got work to do on myself.

My Buddhist teacher memorably says that 'the thought of liking problems should arise as naturally as the thought of liking ice cream'. Treating problems as an opportunity to learn can take away much of their sting. It's also a reminder that they don't just exist 'out there'. When something happens that we don't like, our minds easily slip into panic and exaggeration out of all proportion to the original difficulty, which delays the process of sorting the problem out.

Imagine a world where every problem is welcomed, even if not as ice cream, then as an opportunity for developing understanding of ourselves and others.

Let's pray that we can each approach

one difficulty we encounter today,

not as a cause of irritation and anger,

but as a source of insight and strength.

On Struggling with Doubt and Fear

Mark Wakelin

The Reverend Dr Mark Wakelin is a Methodist Minister in Epsom and a regular presenter of The Daily Service *on Radio 4. He was President of the Methodist Conference from 2012 to 2013.*

Sometimes you only realize what really matters when you hit a significant bump in life's road!

Priorities can change when, for example, you get poorly – with worry, hospital visits, medications and what are euphemistically called 'procedures' that leave you anxious and wary of anyone wearing rubber gloves. In the quieter moments you may wonder at how much energy you've put into some things that seemed so important to you, and regret far more important things that somehow got pushed aside.

Immediately after Jesus's baptism, he goes into the wilderness for a long time. All his priorities are questioned here, all his hopes and dreams, his longings for what might be and what part he might play in that. It's not difficult to imagine the anguish and the heartache of such a difficult time, and to notice the similarity with the painful struggle in the Garden of

Gethsemane. Jesus stands for all of us who have ever been in that lonely place of worry and fear.

None of us welcomes the wilderness or the hard times, and yet sometimes it's only through struggle that we find ourselves and also find God, bringing us strength and hope. I know at other times suffering seems to be nothing but a negative thing, grinding us down and apparently defeating our hope with generous amounts of despair – but not always. And perhaps surprisingly often, it is in the 'garden of tears' or the 'wilderness place' that, despite and through our struggle, we find clarity about what matters.

Lord Jesus,

you know what true temptation means and,

like us, you struggled with doubts and fear.

Help us at such times to notice

the things that really matter

and give us hope for the future.

Amen.

On the Rights and Wrongs of Anger

Janet Wootton

The Reverend Dr Janet Wootton is Director of Learning and Development for the Congregational Federation. She is on the editorial team for Feminist Theology *journal and* Worship Live.

Any devotee of the cryptic crossword will have come across the near-anagrams around the words *anger*, *angered*, *enraged* and *danger*. And know that the same letters can spell *endanger* and *end anger*. All very useful to the crossword compilers.

These words resonate in the English language because of their closeness in spelling and sound. We can see the danger that anger causes: road rage, violence in the home, street fights fuelled by alcohol and drugs. And we also see the fractures in human society along whose edges we rage against one another's moral values, race or religion.

So could we end anger? It is the seductive message in the lyrics of John Lennon's song 'Imagine'. Nothing to kill or die for, and – for good measure in today's violence-torn world – no religion too.

But perhaps to end anger might endanger something about our humanity.

I am quick to become angry – I wish I was not, as I end up upsetting people and having to apologize. But I am also grateful for slow-burning anger against poverty and injustice and abuse, because it provides the impulse and the energy to do something about them.

There are things in this world to which the only rational response is powerful anger: not a thirst for revenge, nor the desire to harm the perpetrators, but the power to speak out against wrong and put things right.

This is recognized in a surprising verse from a hymn about Jesus by John Bell and Graham Maule, in which Jesus is described as 'raging' against injustice, and the singer is invited to rage with him in the cause of good.

God,

may our anger never endanger

our relationships or the lives of others.

But may steadfast rage right wrong,

in Your power and Your love.

Amen.

On Despair and Hope

Peter Baker

The Reverend Peter Baker, former Senior Pastor of Highfields Church, Cardiff, took over as Senior Minister of Lansdowne Baptist Church, Bournemouth, in 2013.

'Why are you downcast, O my soul? Why so disturbed within me?' Such honesty may surprise those who imagine that belief in God places us beyond the possibility of personal despair and doubt. Not so. The Psalms, from which that opening quotation comes, are refreshingly real – they sing it and pray it the way that it so often is in our lives.

Psalm 42 is written out of an experience of the most intense sadness of heart. 'My tears have been my food day and night,' the Psalmist comments; and then continues: 'Deep calls to deep in the roar of your waterfalls; all your waves and breakers have swept over me.'

These symptoms sound very similar to what we tend to describe as depression. That is, of course, a complex and common condition. And as the Psalm reminds us, faith does not make us immune to such overwhelming feelings of vulnerability and disorientation. Life on the ragged edge can be the experience of us all, including those who believe in God.

This is why it can be so unhelpful to tell people to 'snap out of it!' We are multi-dimensional creatures in whom the various aspects of our being constantly interact. And our health, therefore, will usually be the product of treating symptoms at all those levels.

According to the Psalm, faith in God gives the capacity to talk to oneself without listening only to the negative voices of life. We're able to separate the inner person from the outer, which is the product of environment, heredity and circumstance. This soul-speak is the route to well-being. Which is why the Psalmist can address himself positively in conclusion: 'Soul, put your hope in God, for I will yet praise Him, my Saviour and my God.'

Lord,

be with all who struggle

with the disorientation of their life.

And may we each learn the importance of

talking to as well as listening to ourselves.

Amen.

On Learning from Our Mistakes

Frances Finn

Frances Finn is a journalist and presenter for TV and radio, including on The Daily Service *on BBC Radio 4. She has written movingly about a serious motorbike accident that hospitalized her in 2009.*

It was 6.30 in the evening, and 15 million people watched as a BBC journalist was handbagged into history. There was John Sergeant, clad in his usual grey raincoat, on the steps of the British Embassy in Paris. He told the nation that Margaret Thatcher had failed to win enough support to stay as Conservative party leader and there must be another round of voting. This was not something she would come out and comment on, he said confidently. And with the timing of a well-rehearsed pantomime, the door behind him opened. 'Mrs Thatcher is behind you,' said Peter Sissons from the studio. As John turned to look, the Iron Lady tangoed him out of position to address the microphones that had sprung up into shot.

Looking back on those events, the BBC's former chief political correspondent says it was the making of his career. He says he was hardly noticed until his mistake on that evening in November 1990. He went on to become a household name.

As someone who's no stranger to making mistakes, I do enjoy hearing stories of success born out of failure. Failures are so rarely tolerated in public life.

I'm thankful that the God I follow is a fan of second chances. The Bible's full of stories of people who are called to do jobs, who mess up, but then go on to do even greater things. Even St Peter lied three times about knowing Jesus. For him, there was not only forgiveness and restoration, but transformation into something better than before. As one church leader puts it, 'God can make a winning hand out of a pair of twos!'

Lord,

give me the humility

to learn from my bad decisions.

Thank You that when we ask You,

You give a fresh start after each mistake.

Bless our work and make it fruitful,

in Jesus' name,

Amen.

On Trusting in the Darkness

Martyn Atkins

The Reverend Dr Martyn Atkins is the Superintendent Minister and Team Leader at Methodist Central Hall, Westminster, and formerly the General Secretary of the Methodist Church in Britain.

The Diet of Worms reached a critical point in 1521. This reference is not to the latest fad in weight loss, but to the questioning of a young monk. A Diet was a formal gathering to deliberate and pronounce upon matters relating to the Holy Roman Empire; Worms was the place in Germany where this took place, and the monk in question was called Martin Luther.

Luther's various publications, including the famous '95 Theses', were placed on a table and he was asked to revoke the heresies they were said to contain. He asked for time to reflect and on 18 April reappeared before the court where the same question was put to him: 'Will you recant?'

His response – sometimes rendered 'Here I stand, I can do no other' – is one of the great speeches of history.

'Unless I am convinced by the testimony of the Scriptures or by clear reason,' he said, 'I am bound by the Scriptures I have quoted and my conscience is captive to the Word of God. I cannot and will not recant anything, since it is neither safe nor right to go against conscience. May God help me.'

Yet Luther was, for all his courage and greatness, one who suffered from mental illnesses, clinging to God and to faith in the depths and darkness. Here is one of his prayers:

Behold, Lord,

an empty vessel that needs to be filled.

My Lord, fill it. I am weak in the faith;

strengthen me. I am cold in love; warm me

and make me fervent, that my love may go out

to my neighbour. I do not have a strong faith;

at times I doubt. O Lord, help me.

Strengthen my faith and trust in You.

With me, there is an abundance of sin;

in You is the fullness of righteousness.

Therefore I will strive to remain with You.

Amen.

On Finding God in Times
of Suffering

Andrew Martlew

*Father Andrew Martlew is a former Army Chaplain who is now Vicar
of St Martin's, Womersley, in North Yorkshire, and an Honorary
Chaplain of York Minster.*

LET NOTHING DISTURB YOU

St Peter's Basilica in Rome is an awe-inspiring building. It's probably the biggest cathedral in the world. It's full of magnificent altars and statues and gold and mosaics and people – great swirls of them which, at least for me, do nothing to detract from the magnificence of the building and its role as a reminder of the majesty of God.

Tucked away in a side-chapel, behind an armoured glass screen, is one of the great sculptural masterpieces of the Renaissance: Michelangelo's *Pietà*, commissioned in 1498. Mary cradles the body of her dead son on her lap. She is young and beautiful. He is barely marked by crucifixion. Polished, glowing marble – a mere five-and-a-half feet high, even though in my mind's eye it's on the same magnificent scale as the Basilica itself. An object of perfect beauty both in form and content.

And every time I see it, ever so quietly I weep. Somehow this thing of beauty speaks to me not just of the pain and desolation of Mary, but of the grief of every mother who has ever held her dead son. And through her, it speaks to me of the suffering of the whole of humanity, and therefore also of the presence of God at the very centre of that suffering.

Heavenly Father,

You are with us at all times,

in sorrow, in sickness and in poverty;

hold us in Your loving arms though

the world seems full of sorrow and pain,

and cradle us as we struggle

toward our home with You.

In Jesus's name we pray.

Amen.

On Honouring Old Age

Edward Kessler

Dr Edward Kessler MBE *is an author and the Founding Director of*
The Woolf Institute, Cambridge. He is a notable thinker in interfaith
relations and Fellow of St Edmund's College.

Sometimes our lives are darkened by the fear of ageing. By bleaching our hair, lifting our faces and dressing in fashionable clothes, we hope to stay young forever – to ward off the inevitability of death. We hope that by joking about Zimmer frames and care homes we will keep them at a distance. Worse, we treat the old without respect; we do not consider them to have a view, to be of relevance. They are a spent commodity. A burden.

There is one way to prevent the encroachment of death into the realm of life, and that is by truly living each day, by refusing to view ageing as equivalent to dying.

We can honour the old among us. Look at Moses and his brother, Aaron, who appear before Pharaoh to demand the freedom of the Israelites. In what looks like an unnecessary digression, the Book of Exodus records that 'Moses was 80 years old and Aaron was 83, when they made their demand on Pharaoh'.

Why does the Bible reveal something so mundane as their ages? Because old age is a source of pride. In the words of the Talmud, '80 – the age of strength'. What is the strength of 80 years? Surely a teenager is stronger?

But the strength of 80 is the wisdom that comes from experience and completion. Having run much of the course of life, having seen the follies and passions of the human heart rise and subside, having seen their own and their friends' dreams fulfilled or disappointed, an adult of 80 years is finally able to look at the human condition with proper scepticism and compassion.

We pray that in old age

God may plant us like cedars

in the divine courtyard.

Amen.

On Having the Courage
to Do Good

Ranjit-Singh Dhanda

Ranjit-Singh Dhanda is Lead for Faith Inclusion across the Nishkam Schools, guided by Bhai Sahib Bhai Dr Mohinder Singh Ji. Previously, he was the Sikh Chaplain to Wolverhampton University.

Even at the age of 56, I find the closing supplication of every Sikh prayer a huge challenge. All Sikh prayers end with the reminder that God's Name is forever in ascendance and it is God's Will that everyone is forgiven and blessed. We're called upon to forgive and seek God's blessings for all, without discrimination. To live out this closing prayer requires enormous spiritual strength.

In the Sikh tradition there exists the concept of the *sant sipaahi*, or 'saint-soldier' – one who has the courage and fortitude to do good in the face of seemingly and quite possibly insurmountable problems. So where is this battlefield and what is the conflict?

The battlefield and conflict are in fact one: the mind. Becoming saintly and doing good deeds to gain spiritual strength is the easy bit. That spiritual strength is required to keep doing good in adversity, to control one's own mind and to save it from the vices of anger, lust, greed, materialistic attachment and arrogance.

It is only once this mind is composed and at peace, having the spiritual strength to win these internal battles, that we can sincerely ask for the Lord's forgiveness and blessings for all from the heart.

Please Lord,

bless our political leaders

and each and every one of us

with the spiritual strength, humility

and wisdom to act with nobility.

Let us all contribute selflessly and tirelessly

toward achieving peace for all.

On Hitting the Wall and Keeping Going

Cathy Le Feuvre

Cathy Le Feuvre is a writer and broadcaster, currently based at BBC Radio Jersey. She has previously worked as a media consultant, including seven years in the media office of The Salvation Army.

The countdown had begun. For many thousands of people, the preparation was over. The long winter months of training were behind them. Tomorrow they would line up for the London Marathon.

I'm always amazed by this spectacular event. The sheer determination of the runners is astonishing. Of course, the elite athletes – the top marathon runners in the world – are always there, and we expect to see them at their best. But lining up for the same event are many more for whom this activity is not a full-time career: those running for fun, for charity, to beat their own best times.

I'm informed by friends braver than me who have completed the London Marathon that for many runners there's a moment in the race when they 'hit the wall'. This is the point when it's tempting to look back at the vast distance already travelled and think 'I've had enough!'

But it's then, I'm told, when it's important not to think of the miles already completed but to look ahead and anticipate the end of the journey. To plough on, break through the pain and complete the race.

St Paul, writing to early Christians in Philippi, used the analogy of a race to encourage them not to give up on their faith. 'I've got my eye on the goal, where God is beckoning us onward – to Jesus,' he says. 'I'm off and running and I'm not turning back!'

Lord,

at times it's tempting to give up on life,

especially when things are getting tough.

Help us not to dwell on past mistakes or

setbacks but to start again today

to look forward with optimism

into the future with You.

Amen.

On Knowing That All Things Pass

George Stack

The Most Reverend George Stack was installed as Archbishop of Cardiff in 2011. He has also been Administrator of Westminster Cathedral and Auxiliary Bishop in the Archdiocese of Westminster.

With its music, culture and extraordinary history, I've long been fascinated by Spain. The fortress town of Ávila in Castile is quite spectacular. It was there that the great St Teresa persuaded St John of the Cross to become her spiritual director. Together they followed the mystical path called the 'Ascent to Nothingness'.

This teaches that God is all, and a life which is already overcrowded cannot receive the fullness of God's gift. So the challenge of this teaching is to empty ourselves of those things we think give identity, security and meaning to our lives.

In that emptiness, we'll discover the things of God. St John of the Cross described this as *nada*, nothing. Let nothing come between yourself and the ground of your being – God Himself.

The greatness of John's mystical path lies in his objective, heroic, analytical and rational approach to the subject. He avoids the extremes of emotion which promise heaven or threaten hell. He invites Teresa and those who follow him to realize that nothing is lost and all is gained in opening the depth of our being to the presence and the love of God.

So, a prayer of St Teresa:

Let nothing disturb thee,

Let nothing dismay thee.

All things pass.

God never changes.

Patience attains

All that it strives for.

He who has God

Lacks for nothing.

God alone suffices.

Amen.

ON KNOWING THAT ALL THINGS PASS

A World of Wonder

When we stop and really *look* at the world around
us, we open ourselves to its beauty and to God's love.
The mystery and miracle of creation are apparent
whether our focus is on the multitudes of stars in
the night sky or on a tiny insect that has landed on a
flower. This chapter reflects on the moments in which
we perceive the beauty, wonder and love in our world.
There are meditations on the human face, on the joy
inspired by childhood innocence, on our kinship with
animals, and on the uplifting art and music inspired by
our divine imagination. The prayers here enlarge our
minds and hearts in a spirit of profound gratitude for
the manifold blessings of existence.

On Being Surprised

Jeremy Morris

The Reverend Dr Jeremy Morris is Master of Trinity Hall, having been Dean of Trinity Hall and then of King's College, Cambridge. He is a Fellow of the Royal Historical Society, and a Church of England priest.

Recently I had a family holiday on the west coast of Scotland. Unfortunately we had one of those washed-out weeks when it seemed never to stop raining, and everyone was grumpy and wanted to go home. But there was one highlight, a daytrip to the abbey on Iona, when, just as the ferry across to the island got under way, the sun came out and we had three hours of glorious weather.

In those three hours the world, and our week, were transformed. The sea was a glorious, deep blue. And life was good after all.

Since then, I've thought much about the suddenness of beauty, how it catches us off-guard sometimes, as if we're suddenly shown something in a new light. Those monks must have worked or prayed through the long, wet, dark hours of winter, only to look up sometimes and see, with new eyes, the radiance with which God had clothed the world around them.

I've often heard people say that Iona is a special place. And yet most of us are stuck with city life, with traffic jams, delayed trains, overdue bills, the school run or the pressing deadline. We're like the monks, face down, jaws set, pressing on with what we must do.

It's hard sometimes to see the beauty around us, not only in places and buildings and nature, but in people and the things they do and say. Perhaps we could hold up our heads a bit more often and look more closely. Perhaps we could allow ourselves to be surprised by our world.

Help us to see our world with Your eyes,

Lord, so that we may learn the pattern

of Your love, and knowing it,

we may be strengthened to follow it,

all our days.

Amen.

On the Mystery of the Human Face

Musharraf Hussain

Dr Musharraf Hussain OBE *is a scientist, educator and religious scholar. He is Chief Executive of the Karimia Institute, Chief Editor of* The Invitation, *and Vice Chair of the Christian/Muslim Forum.*

In the name of God, the most merciful, the most kind.

When travelling on the London Underground during the rush hour I am always fascinated by the multitude of faces – an ocean of humanity: white, brown, black, pink, round faces, long ones, and yet all beautiful in their own way. Undoubtedly, the human face is an artistic achievement: the icon of God's creation. The face is the mirror of the mind. On this quite compact but complex shape an amazing array of feelings can be expressed: joy, excitement, ecstasy, sadness, sorrow, bereavement, disgust, annoyance, love. There is always a special variation of presence in each one. Each face is unique: no two are exactly the same.

A world lies hidden behind each face. Momentary looks can lead to a gaze of recognition, or of questioning as strangers pass each other – or even to a conversation. In some faces the vulnerability of the person within is obvious – an inner turbulence finding its way to the surface. Then there's the human face that carries mystery – perhaps where the private inner world projects outward. It might only be a smile that calls for understanding and compassion from you or me. That smile from the inner world of the individual can bring such joyous illumination!

The Prophet of Islam taught, 'Meet people with a cheerful face and display good character.' And he also said, 'a smile is charity.'

O Loving God,

open our hearts and minds

so that we may do good

that will bring smiles

to the faces of others.

Amin.

On the Example of Children

Judy Merry

The late Judy Merry was a freelance producer and presenter, having worked for many years in BBC Children's Television. She was also a lecturer in journalism at UCLan in Preston.

I visited a children's hospice recently – not to see the children who have limited life expectancy, but to look at the work of a group that tries to help their siblings. When you think about a hospice for children, you immediately think of a child who will almost certainly not reach adulthood. But perhaps we don't give much thought to the other children in the family.

It doesn't take much imagination to realize that the parents often concentrate on the needs of the ill child. But life is very tough for their brothers and sisters.

For instance, I hadn't thought about how difficult it is to get a wheelchair onto a beach – so a simple visit to the seaside is rarely possible. That's why the hospice took the children there for a day out. One little brother was asked what was the best part of the day. It wasn't being able to paddle in the sea or looking for crabs in rock pools. It was – in his words – 'having Mum to myself'.

Children get a great deal of criticism these days – and I don't think I'd have blamed these particular children if they'd shown a great deal of resentment at the limitations which circumstances had put on their lives. But when I talked to them, what struck me was the way they put the needs of others before their own.

They know they can't have the attention from their parents that other children get. One teenager said he didn't talk to his family about his worries, because he didn't want to upset them – and a nine-year-old boy didn't seem to resent his brother at all. He said, 'I really love him,' and spoke passionately about how angry he got if anyone stared at his brother or called him names.

Jesus implied that we have a great deal to learn from young children. They have little status – and yet they often behave better than the adults around them.

Lord,

give us the humility to admit that

children can often teach us the way to live.

Help us to see the needs of others and know

that there are times when someone else's needs

must come before our own.

Amen.

On the Dawn Chorus

Michael Ford

The Reverend Dr Michael Ford, a former BBC journalist, is an author of books on contemporary Christian spirituality. He is a specialist in the work of the Dutch pastoral theologian Henri JM Nouwen.

There's nothing more spiritually uplifting at this time of the year than the sound of the dawn chorus, a mystery of creation that begins in March and reaches its peak in May. Blackbirds, robins, wrens, warblers, thrushes and finches – all take part in an earthly ritual received as heavenly melody.

Birds sing, of course, with the very practical purpose of defending their territory or attracting a mate, and they do so particularly at dawn when the air is still and sound transmission is at its best. Some people might find the symphony wakes them up far too early but, for me, lying in bed and praying with the chorus involves me in a liturgical act that seems to purify the past and sanctify the day ahead – a holy communion with creation that has the power of a sacrament to heal and transform.

ON THE DAWN CHORUS

The French composer and ornithologist Olivier Messiaen believed birds to be the greatest musicians. Notating their songs across the world, he incorporated transcriptions into most of his music, which was often a theological explosion of joy, divine love and redemption. For him, birdsong symbolized the presence of God in creation. 'In the domain of music,' he said, 'birds have discovered everything. If birds are the source of all earthly music, then as musical symbols of creation they are also messengers of heavenly music.'

O Lord, our Sovereign,

how majestic is Your name in all the earth.

You have set Your glory above the heavens.

Help us to perceive the divine mystery

at the heart of all creation

and be renewed by it.

Amen.

On Connecting with the Animal Kingdom

Jeremy Morris

The Reverend Dr Jeremy Morris is Master of Trinity Hall, having been Dean of Trinity Hall and then of King's College, Cambridge. He is a Fellow of the Royal Historical Society, and a Church of England priest.

Not so long ago, for the first time in my life, I became the owner of a pet dog, a cross-breed terrier. He's a lovely pet for the family. And I love my dog. That is, I love this particular dog – perhaps not dogs in general.

I'm wary of the way we can get too sentimental about animals. But at the same time, my dog has a character I adore. I know it's a mistake to think of him in terms that are too human. But he has personality, loyalty, affection, unpredictability and playfulness.

Animals can connect with us. There's an ancient Christian argument about whether animals have souls. I think they probably do. There is, surely, something in them – however remote it may seem sometimes – that strikes a chord in us, and evokes our sympathy.

We all need to be reminded of our connectedness to animals. God has placed us in a world rich with colour and variety. We know, of course, that it's a harsh world, in which – so we say – dog eats dog. The terrier whose affection I admire is also the terrier who would savage small birds and squirrels, given half a chance.

But the world of nature is greater than us, and we're one small link in its chain. Pets remind us of that. The harsh way of nature shouldn't blind us to its beauties.

Awaken in us, Lord,

a growing appreciation of the infinite richness

of our world, and of all the many creatures

it contains, that we may learn to treasure

and protect them, now and always.

Amen.

On Seeing God in the Ordinary

Peter Townley

The Venerable Peter Townley is Archdeacon of Pontefract. He spent the first 16 years of his ministry in the Manchester area. Before moving to Pontefract, he was Vicar of St Mary le Tower, Ipswich.

St James the Great has always been special to me, because I was baptised at St James the Great in Collyhurst in Manchester one snowy December afternoon. For many others, St James is important because his remains are in the Cathedral at Santiago de Compostela, which is now, more than ever, a popular pilgrimage destination.

St James is well known for two stories in the Gospels. The first is that of James and his brother John's anxious mother and her wish that her two sons are given the best seats in the Kingdom of God. Jesus firmly reminds her that the Christian life is about service rather than status. The other is his mountain-top experience with John and Peter of seeing Jesus transfigured.

Reading those stories through the eyes of St James turns our world-view upside down so that we see God and each other in a new way.

This dramatically happened to Charles Raven (1885–1964), a great theologian in his day, who was something of a mystic. One of his life-changing experiences happened as he passed a chip shop in Liverpool.

He talked of God meeting him in splendour there. 'I was coming home,' he said, 'and passed some shawl-clad women gathered round a dingy shop.

'The proprietor, in his shirt sleeves, was dispensing packets of fish and chips wrapped in a newspaper. The place was lit by naphtha flares, and misty with the steam of cooking … And again of a sudden the glory; and God fulfilling his eternal task and giving to his children their daily bread.'

Father,

help us to understand You in a new way

and to see Your glory today in

everyday things.

Amen.

On the Recovery of Beauty

Eugene O'Neill

Father Eugene O'Neill is Parish Priest in Belfast, as well as a spiritual director. He contributes regularly to broadcasting and print in the UK, Ireland and the US.

After his visit to Britain, Pope Benedict was reported to have been astonished at the beauty of the Anglican liturgy he witnessed at Westminster Abbey.

It was the spiritual depth and richness of the English choral tradition that moved him; and from this came his invitation to Westminster Abbey choir to sing in Rome at one of the most important events in the Catholic Church's year: the Mass on the Feast Day of St Peter and St Paul.

At this liturgy, newly created archbishops are given 'palliums' – woollen scarves emblazoned with crosses – worn as a symbol of unity with the Pope. Indeed, until the Reformation, the Archbishop of Canterbury himself wore a pallium – a tradition echoed in his coat of arms in which a pallium still appears as a heraldic device.

That England's foremost abbey – itself dedicated to St Peter – should send its celebrated choir to St Peter's Basilica seems wonderfully apt. Around 1,400 years ago, the then pope – St Gregory the Great – was prompted to send St Augustine to re-evangelize England after seeing British boys captured from the Angle tribe in the Roman slave market. Tradition holds that he remarked: 'They are not Angles – but angels.'

This is a remarkable statement of friendship by the Anglican Church; and from the Pope, a sign of a desire to receive from the Anglican tradition.

A sense of beauty is often linked to a craving for immortality; and Pope Benedict has often argued that a recovery of beauty will go hand in hand with recovery of belief in God.

Creator of heavenly harmony,

through music You communicate something

essential, and feed the soul;

may music's angelic beauty humble us

and draw us out of ourselves toward You.

Amen.

On Recognizing the Gift
of Strangers

Sarah Joseph

Sarah Joseph lectures on Islam both within the UK and internationally. In 2004 she was awarded the OBE for services to interfaith dialogue and the promotion of women's rights.

Some of my favourite stories from the Qur'an relate to the Prophet Joseph. When I was younger, I'm sure it was the biblical stories of his rainbow cloak that I loved, or maybe it was because he was my namesake, but as an adult it's Joseph as an outcast, a victim of human trafficking, a refugee, that has inspired me.

Joseph was persecuted by his own kin, and left in a well to die. Traders found him and sold him on as a slave, and thus he was taken from his own land and found himself in Egypt. Handsome and educated, he was purchased by a wealthy merchant, but when Joseph rejected the advances of the merchant's wife, he was cast into prison and forgotten. There he interpreted the dreams of prisoners, and it is one of these men who mentioned Joseph to the King. Joseph was brought before His Majesty, interpreted his dream and stored the grain in a time of abundance, which saved Egypt in a subsequent time of famine. Through this he was able to save his own family who later came to Egypt looking for food.

The story reminds me of so many refugees I've met in my life – people who have been forced from their own lands because of war or persecution, and ended up in Europe and America. Their stories of the persecution from which they fled and the prejudice they have often received have been both inspirational and painful to hear. I remember, 30 years ago, there was a Polish boy at school who fled the then Communist regime with his family. He worked so hard to learn English and to study. He is a scientist now.

Our Lord,

allow us to welcome strangers,

treat them kindly and understand that they

can benefit us as well as those in the lands

from which they come.

Amin.

On the Importance of
Being in Awe

Anna Magnusson

*Anna Magnusson has produced, written and broadcast programmes
for the BBC for more than 25 years. She is the author of three books of
non-fiction.*

There's a Gerard Manley Hopkins poem called 'The Starlight Night' that begins: 'Look at the stars! look, look up at the skies!'

It always pops into my head on cold, black nights when the stars are glittering, or when there's an impossibly bright moon hanging above the houses. The words are perfect: they capture how it feels – that rush of wonder and excitement – when you look up into the vastness, and are caught between worlds: the earth under your feet, the infinite universe beyond.

No doubt that's a bit purple for astronauts and astronomers, but the fact is, it's the looking up beyond the here and now that drew us into space in the first place. It's what took us to the moon, built the space shuttles and launched the Mir space station. For 15 years, Mir orbited the Earth more than 86,000 times. Russian, and later American, astronauts lived on board for months on end. They even raised the first crop of wheat to be grown from seed in outer space.

That compulsion to venture into the unknown – it came out of confidence and energy and vision. Today it sometimes feels as if our heads are bowed, and we don't look up so much. It's hard to see past what's right in front of us in this world: economic turmoil, people and countries struggling to pay their way and survive. Travelling to Mars seems a bit irrelevant when people can't borrow money to buy a house down the road.

And yet, we still feel the tug of the infinite, we still need to look up and be awed by the created universe.

And as we look,

may we know the presence of God,

who is beyond us and within us,

now and forever.

Amen.

On Touching the Infinite

Jenny Wigley

The Reverend Canon Jenny Wigley is Rector of Radyr, on the outskirts of Cardiff. She is a former teacher, whose ministry in the Church in Wales has included university chaplaincy and theological education.

In January Christians celebrate the feast of the Epiphany, the visit of the Wise Men to present their gifts to the Christ-child. They are travellers who come from a place that *we* don't know – somewhere in 'the East' – to a place that *they* don't know – first to Jerusalem and then to Bethlehem, one the birth place and the other the royal seat of David, Israel's most celebrated king. But the Wise Men were in search of the future, not the past, seeking the one the carol calls 'Great David's greater son'.

For many pilgrims today, a place is made holy by its rootedness in the past. They kneel in reverence in a building like my own parish church, where God has been worshipped for centuries. It is, as TS Eliot says, a place 'where prayer has been valid'.

Or it can be the landscape itself that offers that experience. Bardsey Island, off the west coast of Wales, is said to be the burial place of 20,000 saints. It's what the Celtic Christians called a 'thin place', where the divine and natural worlds are so close together that we can catch a glimpse of God beyond the veil that elsewhere hides Him from our sight.

The Celts used to say that heaven and earth are only three feet apart, but in the 'thin' places the distance is much smaller. For the Wise Men in the Gospel story, heaven came so near that they could reach out and touch it. For Christians, God had come to earth in the form of a tiny babe.

Holy God,

Your love enfolds us;

You are before us and behind;

You are the light that shines in our darkness.

Hear our prayer that those who seek You

may find You, and those who find You

may rejoice in that knowledge always;

in the name of Jesus Christ,

who is the Way, the Truth and the Life.

Amen.

STRIVING FOR GOD

This chapter explores the times in our daily lives
when we seek to move closer to God, to transcend our
material existence and glimpse something of heaven
on earth. The opening prayer, offering reflections
on fasting during Ramadan, is a plea for help in
preparing well for this life and the life to come; the
closing prayer, prompted by thoughts of Hanukkah,
calls for 'faith, grace and humility' that will equip
us to do good in the world. In between are inspiring
discussions of the qualities we need to live a more,
meaningful, fulfilling, spiritual life.

On Preparing for Eternity

Ibrahim Mogra

Shaykh Ibrahim Mogra, an Imam from Leicester, promotes national and international interfaith collaboration. He is the founder and Principal of Khazinat al-'Ilm, Madaris of Arabic and Muslim Life Studies.

Fasting in Ramadan is regarded as one of the Pillars of Islam. It is a unique act of sincere obedience to God. It is as if one is living like God who does not eat and drink at all. The degree of sincerity in this act of worship cannot be matched in any other kind of worship. When any person prays in company, others around them can see that they are praying. Their sincerity may be questionable. When any person performs a pilgrimage, others around them can see them. Their sincerity may be questionable. However, no one can tell whether a person is fasting or not. There are no visible signs. Only the fasting person and God know about it. God takes pride in the fasting person and says, 'The fasting is for me and I will personally reward the one who fasts.'

Fasting is like a personal revolution against everyday habits and conventions that enslave people. Before fasting, a person can eat and drink as they please.

When Ramadan comes, it puts a stop to that. Now for a whole month they have to go without food and drink from dawn until sunset. It is as if they are being trained for unforeseen changes in life. Perhaps to be prepared for tougher times. Life is never the same. Circumstances always change. We all have ups and downs: healthy today, ill tomorrow; rich today, poor tomorrow; well fed today, starving tomorrow; self-sufficient today, reliant tomorrow; resident today, traveller tomorrow. Our circumstances change all the time. Ramadan trains us up to face some of these changes and uncertainties of life.

Dear God,

help us to prepare for this life

and the life hereafter.

Amin.

On the Power of Prayer

Martin Shaw

The Right Reverend Martin Shaw served in the Scottish Episcopal Church as the Bishop of Argyll and The Isles from 2004 to 2009. He was also Chaplain to King's College, Cambridge.

There's a lady I know in the Outer Hebrides, who has dedicated herself to praying intensively for refugees all over the world, escaping from hunger or violence, or both. She lives an ordinary, indeed a hidden life. When I asked her about it, she simply said that it was her job. As I left her, she reminded me that if I was going to speak about her work, I must not use her name. Whether or not her prayer is of much use, is not the point.

At the end of her novel *Middlemarch*, in praise of ordinary and maybe insignificant people, George Eliot refers to them as: 'the number who lived faithfully a hidden life, and rest in unvisited tombs.' Thomas Merton, a monk and writer on prayer, wrote an imaginary story of twelve seemingly ordinary people, who don't know each other. Each in their hidden lives holds their arms up, as if they were pillars stopping the world from collapsing. I like to think of them as incognito saints …

Well, someone reading this right now may be one of them and, through prayer, may be stopping the world from falling apart.

Most of us are ordinary and today will come nowhere near an important person, never mind *be* one. The paradox is that the ordinary, hidden people among us perhaps have a huge responsibility. You and I might as well pray, and who knows what the effect might be.

God of unnoticed loving,

Your Presence in those who pray in secret

for others is essential for creation and for the

world's survival. Although their tombs may go

unvisited, we thank You for their hidden lives

which, somehow, have touched and inspired

us to join their loving of others.

Amen.

On Freeing Our Imagination

Stephen Oliver

The Right Reverend Stephen Oliver is the retired Anglican Bishop of Stepney. A former Senior Producer in BBC Religious Broadcasting, he has also been Rector of Leeds and a Canon of St Paul's Cathedral.

I've just come back from Geneva and a visit to the Large Hadron Collider where scientists recreate conditions that existed within a billionth of a second of the Big Bang. Einstein once said that he believed imagination was more important than knowledge. And I can see that. I'm not sure I understand half of what I was told in Geneva, but I suspect my failure was not so much the lack of knowledge as the limits of my imagination. But I have to say that I get excited by science and new ways of understanding the universe.

We often think that science moves forward by the onward march of inexorable logic. But history suggests that progress is by way of that 'Eureka!' moment, the leap of imagination.

Imagination is the foundation of human compassion: the capacity to imagine what someone else is going through. Imagination is what inspires art, which in turn fires my imagination. When David Hockney painted purple trees, it seemed surreal but it made me look at trees more closely and, yes, I began to see the colours he had seen. Imagination is what fuels vision and, for good or ill, human ambition.

For when I came away from Geneva, I realized that what had impressed me most was not so much the basic science as the fact that someone had the vision to build this instrument at all; and more than that, had harnessed the imaginative collaboration of 10,000 scientists and engineers from over 100 countries to build it and make it work. Now that is a miracle.

God of mystery and majesty,

free us from all that constrains imagination

and limits our dreams.

By Your Spirit, illuminate our minds and

expand our vision for a better world

and safe future for all people.

Amen.

On Reflecting God in
Our Endeavours

Tina Beattie

Tina Beattie is an author and the Director of the Digby Stuart Research Centre for Religion, Society and Human Flourishing at the University of Roehampton.

At the dawn of history, when something in
the evolutionary process jumped the tracks of
consciousness, the human emerged as a dreaming ape.
Deep in the caves of the world, creatures began to
paint. A species had evolved that could imagine the
world as other than it is, and from that imaginative
leap came the very essence of what it means to be
human. Werner Herzog's film *Cave of Forgotten
Dreams* takes us inside those caves and enables us to
gaze on wondrous images through 30,000 years of our
time on Earth. He brings us face to face with the most
mysterious and haunting questions about the origins
and meaning of human life. Some say those were the
earliest expressions of religious art.

In the Middle Ages the Gothic cathedrals of Europe
were home to some of the world's greatest art. On
9 June 1310, Duccio's altarpiece, the *Maestà*, was
installed in Siena Cathedral amidst great ceremony.

An eyewitness account tells of how the whole city came together for the procession, and the poor received many alms. The centre panel of the altarpiece shows the Virgin enthroned in majesty, holding the infant Christ, surrounded by angels and saints. It's an image of astonishing serenity, gazing out at us across the centuries with an infinite peace.

Art is powerless to change the world, but great art enables us to imagine a *better* world. That's why tyrants and dictators always wage war on the freedom of art. It remains the most primal and creative expression of human freedom. Without it, we're less than human.

Today, we pray for the gift to see the mystery

of God in the beauty of creation,

and to reflect that beauty

in all our artistic endeavours.

Amen.

On Becoming a Holy Fool

Edwin Counsell

Canon Edwin Counsell has been involved in Christian education for
over two decades and is currently Rector of Llantwit Major. He is a
regular contributor to national radio.

It's never nice to be called a fool. It often means that others are laughing at us, rather than with us, and anyone who's dismissed as a fool is typecast as easily led or manipulated and, invariably, becomes the butt of someone else's joke.

I'm reminded of St Basil of Moscow, who gives his name to the iconic cathedral in that city, with the decorated domes and pinnacles that give it the look of an exotic cake! How ironic that the grandeur of the church that bears his name sits in such stark contrast to Basil's life of humility and poverty in the service of the poor and underprivileged.

Back in the fifteenth century, his peers called him a fool for bucking the trend, and challenging his society to remember the needs of others as much as their own needs and, crucially, to do so in the name of Jesus Christ.

Basil's reputation for foolishness didn't stop there. On one notable occasion he apparently chastised Ivan the Terrible for his violence toward others, and for not paying attention in church! The effect on the famous despot must have been startling, though, because Ivan was amongst the mourners who carried Basil's coffin to the cemetery, after he died in 1552.

In a world where many of us worry constantly about the opinions of others and how we might be perceived, it's sometimes no bad thing to hold a line that's different from those around us. Speaking out when we believe things are unfair, or just plain wrong, might make us foolish in the eyes of some, but it can at times be the right thing to do.

So, Lord,

as we remember Basil, the 'fool for Christ',

may we face up to the opportunities and

challenges of our lives and, in so doing, may

we have courage to recognize all that is right,

and act upon it, even when to do so seems

utter foolishness; and may we know that folly

to be the wisdom that flows from Your grace

and the gifts of Your Spirit.

Amen.

On Seeking a Deeper Trust in God

Richard Chartres

The Right Reverend and Right Honourable Richard Chartres KCVO DD
became Bishop of London and Dean of Her Majesty's Chapels Royal in
1995. He retired as Bishop of London in March 2017.

'I do wish I had a faith,' someone said to me this week. They were polite and wistful, but further conversation revealed that they thought that believing in the Resurrection was really just floating off into some never-never land of wishful thinking.

Actually the message of the risen Jesus was very different. He told his friends to go back to their homes; to go back to Galilee where they had first met. They were to re-immerse themselves in ordinary life but to live in the light of Jesus's way of dying and living.

Jesus did not point the way to dropping out into another world. He immersed himself in this world with all its beauty and tragedy. He took flesh and lived among us, but by doing so did not leave this world as he found it. He was not 'otherworldly' or 'this-worldly', but instead taught his friends how to live in a *next*-worldly way.

So the eleven remaining disciples went to Galilee and met with the risen Christ in a mountainous place, and there, as St Matthew says, they worshipped him, but some doubted.

Doubt is not the opposite of faith. We should respect our honest doubts, which often serve to move us forward from an immature, self-serving understanding to a deeper trust in the self-sacrificing love of God.

The opposite of faith is a life locked up in itself, the disengaged and risk-averse life which is in reality a living death.

Father,

deepen our hunger to see Your plan fulfilled

for the spiritual evolution of the whole

human race and for a world at peace

in which there is justice for all humankind

and care for the whole of creation.

Teach us the imperfections of our

understanding and lead us in the way

of Your Son Jesus to worship You

in spirit and in truth.

Amen.

ON SEEKING A DEEPER TRUST IN GOD

On Living a Christ-like Life

Patrick Thomas

*The Reverend Canon Patrick Thomas is the Vicar of Christ Church,
Carmarthen, and Chancellor of St David's Cathedral, Pembrokeshire.
He has published works in both English and Welsh.*

Some people are hit by tragedies that are so sudden and cruel and apparently pointless that they generate the numbness of shock and disbelief, followed by understandable anger and bitterness. On such occasions it is only natural to turn in on ourselves, entering a spiral of depression.

I knew a farmer's wife, a kindly, lively, intelligent woman, who had been hit by just such a tragedy. Her life, which had been full and satisfying, suddenly seemed barren and empty. She sank deeper and deeper into the darkness – and there was nothing that any of her friends could to do to bring her out of it.

And then she found her own solution. She became a home help, looking after some of the elderly housebound people in our scattered rural community. And as she turned outward toward these often vulnerable and lonely men and women, looking after them with patience and kindness, her inner wounds began to heal. The scars would always be there, of course – but her life acquired new purpose and meaning.

One day I called in to see a blind woman with a wonderful sense of humour, called Hannah, who lived in the old people's bungalows. The farmer's wife was there, gently washing Hannah's feet. As I saw her kneeling there, wholly absorbed in the task of caring for someone else, I felt that somehow I was in the presence of Christ himself.

Heavenly Father,

through Your Son You understand

the depths of pain and anguish into which

we are sometimes plunged.

Be with all those who have to face

bereavement, depression and despair.

In our darkest and most desperate moments,

draw us out from getting lost within ourselves,

and help us to respond to the needs

of those around us.

Amen.

On Growing into our Divine Inheritance

Anna Drew

Anna Drew is Director of Communications for the Anglican diocese of Canterbury. A freelance writer and broadcaster, she is passionate about theology and social justice.

It's strange, what we inherit from our parents – height, eye colour, a passion for classic cars or milky tea. Some say, hard as we try, in the end we all turn into our mothers. I find myself tuning into the same radio programmes, worrying about the weather, complaining about the price of petrol. I've even got her hands.

When I was a little girl I was fascinated by Mum's hands – the creases on her knuckles and palms, the softness of the pale, freckly skin and – best of all – the grey-blue mounds of the raised veins on the backs of her hands. And now perfect replicas are sitting on the ends of my arms. Whatever happens, I'll always carry that piece of her with me – and, though they're not supermodel hands, that's really special to me.

Christians often talk about God as 'our Father'. They believe that every single human being holds within them a little of the DNA of God. And that life is about

ON GROWING INTO OUR DIVINE INHERITANCE

trying to grow into this inheritance – to be a bit more like Jesus, day by day.

For me, it's all about the hands. Jesus said, 'My mother and brothers are those who hear the word of God and do it.' I think this is what brings to life the God-blood running through our veins. Getting stuck in to make this world a better place, seeing what needs doing and getting your hands dirty.

And maybe, if we take time to notice that trace of the Divine in others and the shared inheritance that connects us all, we won't be so quick to judge or dismiss. Perhaps we'll be surprised by our shared family resemblance.

Lord of hands and faces, hearts and desires,

give us confidence in our divine inheritance –

and the courage to get our hands dirty.

Amen.

On Walking Humbly with God

Naftali Brawer

*Rabbi Dr Naftali Brawer was ordained as an Orthodox Rabbi aged 22.
He is Rabbi and co-founder of Mishkan, a trans-geographical Jewish
community, as well as a columnist and a published author.*

During the eight days of Hanukkah, the lights are kindled just after sunset, and there is something about dusk and candlelight that I find particularly evocative. Dusk is not day but it is not entirely night either. Soft candlelight illuminates and at the same time conceals, unlike harsh electricity that leaves little to the imagination.

That the Hanukkah ritual is framed in this half-light says something about faith that is all too often overlooked. For many, faith and religion are about certainty in a world of uncertainty. We seek clear boundaries and delineations, immutable truths, and yet our experience is one of turbulence and disorientation.

Some turn to religion to find a bedrock. They want a world that makes sense in black-and-white terms, and fundamentalist religion provides this oversimplification of life. But this is a distortion of what real faith is about. Real faith does not seek to escape from life's complexities by providing simple answers but rather heightens the complexity and makes demands on the adherent to navigate a moral life with nuance and sensitivity. Religion is like the soft light of candles or the natural light of dusk when day mingles with night; it holds opposites in awareness and assumes a stance of wonder and awe toward the deep mysteries of our existence without trying to reduce them to simplistic schemes.

While fundamentalists march through life, a person of true faith treads gingerly, attuned to the subtlety and complexity of life. As the prophet Micah says: 'What does God require of you, but to act justly, to love mercy and to walk humbly with your God.'

Father in heaven,

help us to navigate our complex reality

with faith, grace and humility

so that we may bring blessing

wherever we go.

Index of Contributors

Acknowledgements

The Publishers would like to thank Michael Ford for his invaluable assistance in preparing this book. Thanks also to Sister Catherine Wybourne for writing the Foreword, and to Vanessa Ford at the BBC for her support.